PLANTERS PEANUT ™

1906-1961
COLLECTIBLES
A Handbook and Price Guide

Jan Lindenberger
with Joyce Spontak

77 Lower Valley Road, Atglen, PA 19310

Published by Schiffer Publishing, Ltd.
77 Lower Valley Road
Atglen, PA 19310
Please write for a free catalog.
This book may be purchased from the
publisher.
Please include $2.95 postage.
Try your bookstore first.

We are interested in hearing from
authors
with book ideas on related topics.

Printed in Hong Kong.
ISBN: 0-88740-792-7

Library of Congress Cataloging-in-
Publication Data

Lindenberger, Jan.
    Planter's Peanut collectibles, 1906-1961:
a handbook and price guide/Jan
Lindenberger with Joyce Spontak.
        p.   cm.
    ISBN 0-88740-792-7 (pbk.)
    1. Planters Peanuts (Firm)--
Collectibles--Catalogs. I. Spontak, Joyce.
II. Title.
NK808.L56 1995
338.7'6648056596--dc20   95-10515
                                CIP

Contents

Acknowledgements

Many thanks to Joyce and Robert Spontak. These wonderful people opened up their home and allowed me to photograph their extensive and varied collection. The majority of the information for this book came from these well-informed people. Joyce was once an employee of the Planters Peanut Company.

I really appreciated her patience and the hours of arranging and rearranging her wonderful collection. Especially since it was through the Christmas holidays.

Joyce and Bob have been collecting Mr. Peanut and Planters items for many years. It all started when Joyce's grandmother gave her a plastic bank in the shape of Mr. Peanut. Years later, as an adult, she found a matching cup and then a mechanical pencil. When her husband gave her a large store six-sided jar, she believed she then had every item Planters ever made.

In their active pursuit of Mr. Peanut items, they found out about and joined Peanut Pals, a group of collectors who shared their interests. Since that time their collection has grown considerably. Joyce became editor of the club's bi-monthly newsletter for the next six years. If anyone has any questions or needs information on any Planters item they may contact Joyce at (412) 221-7599 or by mail at 804 Hickory Grade Road, Bridgeville, Pennsylvania. 15017.

Also, many thanks to Van Benedick. Without his help much of this book would not have been possible. Van has been collecting since 1977 and has amassed thousands of items. He opened his home and allowed us to photograph his one-of-a-kind collection. Van was also a wonderful source of pricing and dating items.

Further thanks goes to Arleane Pawlowics, Joe Stivaletti, Marty and Pam Blank, and to anyone else I may have forgotten.

Introduction

The ubiquitous peanut. It conjures up images of baseball and football games, of summer picnics and friends conversing around a cozy fire. From its humble beginnings, the Planters peanut has expanded its range to encompass the world. And in the process, it has created an icon of the advertising industry and an outstanding opportunity for collectors.

In 1889, at age 12, Amedeo Obici arrived in New York from Italy. He had virtually no money and couldn't speak English, yet he was determined to make his own way in this new country. After moving to Wilkes-Barre, Pennsylvania, and a brief bout of formal schooling, he worked at various jobs, including his uncle's fruit stand. In 1896 he bought a peanut roaster and went into business for himself.

After several years of selling peanuts to other shopkeepers from a small store and a horse-drawn cart, in 1906 Obici teamed up with his friend and brother-in-law, Mario Peruzzi, to expand the peanut business. They chose the name Planters for their new partnership, because it sounded important. They rented two floors of a factory in Wilkes-Barre for $25.00 a month. With eight employees they marketed their first product, Burgomaster brand of blanched and salted Virginia peanuts.

At the time, freshly roasted peanuts were a novelty; most nuts were sold in the shell, raw and unsalted. The only other salted nuts available were the small spanish peanuts sold in bulk at 10 cents a pound. Most retailers kept nuts in glass jars and measured out what customers wanted into paper envelopes. Obici and Peruzzi roasted and salted the larger Virginia peanuts and sold them in two-ounce nickel bags. The idea caught on with both their retailers and the public.

Obici constantly looked for ways to improve his product. One concern was keeping the peanuts fresh. To preserve them he packaged them in glassine paper, at first. Later he switched to cellophane paper, then glass jars, and finally to the vacuum-sealed blue tins. In 1913 the Planters Nut and Chocolate Company moved to Suffolk, Virginia, closer to where peanuts were grown, and built its own factory for processing and packaging. Two more plants eventually opened: the San Francisco plant in 1921 and the Toronto, Canada plant in 1925.

Planters Nut and Chocolate Company gained the reputation not only for top quality items, but for being one big family when it came to taking care of their employees. There was no pension plan, but when an employee felt that he ar she was too old to continue working, they were told to enjoy their retirement but to show up each week to continue collecting a paycheck for the rest of their lives. The profit the company made was returned to the employees and to the community in the form of hospitals and educational programs.

Part of Obici's business savvy was a gift for advertising his product. Early in the company's history, he packaged one of the letters from his name in each bag of peanuts; anyone who collected all the letters got a free bag of nuts. Obici realized that the key to his success was repeat sales, and by extension name recognition. So in 1916 Planters held a contest to develop a trademark, offering a prize of $5.00 for the best design. The winner was a 14-year-old boy, who submitted a drawing of a "little peanut person." To enhance the image, a commercial artist later added the top hat, monocle, and cane for a more upscale look. And so Mr. Peanut became part of our heritage.

With a full-page appearance in the Saturday Evening Post in 1918, Mr. Peanut became the first peanut to be nationally advertised. It was the start of an auspicious campaign. Obici believed in using all available advertising and promotional media, and since 1918 Mr. Peanut has been featured virtually on every Planters package, container, and ad. As a result, he has become one of the most familiar figures in advertising, and because of this presence, the opportunities for collectors are virtually endless.

In addition to its extensive container and advertising memorabilia, through the years Planters has offered a variety of premium items with its products. Mugs, pencils, pens, tote bags, and the like are all available

1919

1920

1918

by redeeming product wrappers. This is part of the company's on-going promotion of Mr. Peanut and their products.

Thanks to Obici's flair for innovative marketing, Mr. Peanut can be found on practically every conceivable product; from glass jars to metal tins, from wristwatches to charm bracelets, from ashtrays to clocks, from plastic whistles to display figures with monocles that light up. A special line of souvenir items helped Planters celebrate the 1939 World's Fair.

With this variety of products, it is very easy for collectors to get started with Mr. Peanut. Most paraphernalia sells in the $20 range, but very rare items can run into hundreds and sometimes even thousands of dollars. This handbook and price guide provides information for collectors just starting out, yet will be a valuable reference for those whose collections are in the higher price range as well.

No matter where your collection falls, Mr. Peanut offers a lesson in the possibilities of product advertising and promotion. His smiling face and debonair pose, synonymous with nut products for so many years, today are a fun and important part of the collectibles world.

The items in this book reflect the early years of the Planters Nut and Chocolate Company, 1906-1961. The information and pictures shown here are intended to assist in the knowledge of what items were produced, cost and authenticity. Prices may vary from those listed due to geographic location and condition of the item. The prices are based on cost averaging, not on an isolated sale and definitely not on price tags on unsold items. A price "not available" notation is necessary on some of these items.

1922

1923

1925

1926

**1948
and into
the 1950s**

**1927
to
1945**

1957

MR.
PEANUT
®

**1962
and into
the 1980s**

**PRESENT
1990**

Store Displays and Figurals

Cast iron fence post sitter. Was used for decorating Planters factory roof tops beginning in the 1920s. 38" high. Price not available.

Newer style blinker Mr. Peanut. 1930s. Price not available.

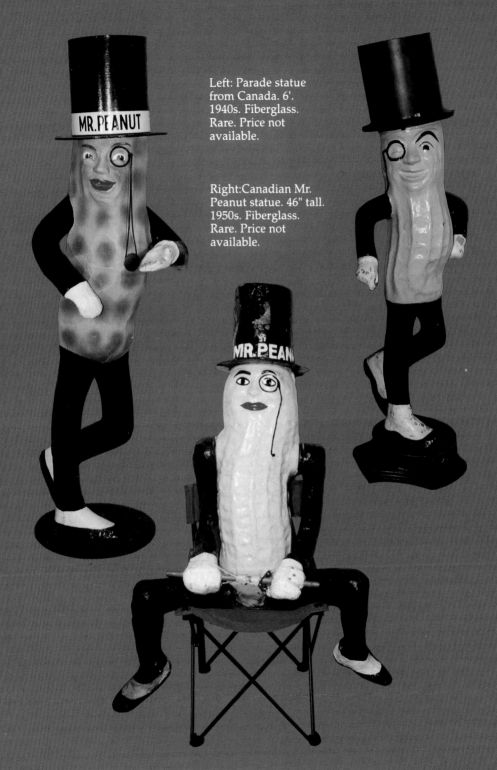

Left: Parade statue from Canada. 6'. 1940s. Fiberglass. Rare. Price not available.

Right:Canadian Mr. Peanut statue. 46" tall. 1950s. Fiberglass. Rare. Price not available.

Roaster rider made of papier mache. 1940s. Rare. Price unavailable.

Penny scale of full-size Mr. Peanut. 1940s. Watch out for reproductions on this item. Very hard to tell. Rare. Price not available.

Cardboard sitting lady holding 5 cent salted peanuts display. 26". 1930s. $450-650.

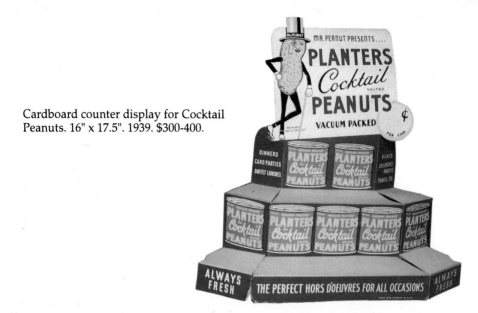

Cardboard counter display for Cocktail
Peanuts. 16" x 17.5". 1939. $300-400.

Electric display piece for Cooking &
Salad Oil. Approximately 4' x 4'. 1950.
Price not available.

Cardboard store display-shipper. 1950s.
$75-100.

Planters metal display rack. 15" x 10.5". 1950s. $15-30.

Metal Planters display rack. 18" x 7.5". 1950s. $30-50.

Metal display rack with Canadian header card. 12" x 17.5". 1950s. Rack $15-30. Card $25-40.

Metal store rack with header sign. 1950. $50-100.

Neon store clock. Electric with green border. 20". 1940. Price not available.

Glass and Ceramic

Glass pedestal jar. The first peanut jar made for Planter in 1922 (the second version has a raised lid), and the original shipping box. Rare. Price not available.

Octagon peanut jar. May be embossed on all eight sides or on seven sides with the eighth side accepting a paper label. 1926. 10.5" without the peanut finial lid. Reproductions are in colors or clear with bad spacing, such as Plante-rs. $60-100.

Tin base display holder for the fish bowl jar. (Base display 7.5" across.) Price not available.

Fishbowl peanut jar. Rectangular label, also found on other jars. 11" without the peanut finial lid. 1929. $60-100.

Fishbowl peanut jar. Horizontal label with 5 cent on label. 11" (without the lid). Has peanut finial on lid. 1929. $60-100.

Fish bowl peanut jar. This version has a T-shaped label. 11", without the peanut finial lid. 1929. $95-150.

Small glass fish globe jar for Planters salted peanuts with original paper label. 1929. $150-250.

Four corner peanut jar. This jar has been reproduced in colors and clear glass. 11.75" without the lid. 1932. $150-250.

Football peanut jar. Has "Planters" embossed across the top of the jar and "Salted Peanuts" across the bottom. 6.625" without the lid. 1930. $125-175.

Square glass peanut jar with paper label and finial peanut on lid. 1934. $100-150.

Square peanut jar with glass peanut finial lid. 7.375" without the lid. "Planters" embossed across the top of the jar. 1934. $40-70.

Glass pickle jar-shaped peanut jar with wire and wood handle. 1936. $200-250.

Barrel peanut jar with Mr. Peanut embossed on jar in different stances. 10" without the peanut finial lid. 1935. This lid is 9" across and is the only large lid jar. Originally came with a label and silver paint on the embossed figures. $150-250.

18

Six-sided jar with peanut finial lid. Has fired-on yellow Mr. Peanut on three sides. Other versions have white "Planters" or no Mr. Peanut. This correct lid has "Planters" embossed on the top and a peanut finial. 7.25" without the lid. 1936. $75-90.

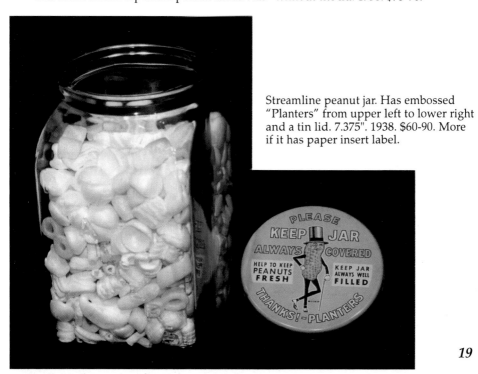

Streamline peanut jar. Has embossed "Planters" from upper left to lower right and a tin lid. 7.375". 1938. $60-90. More if it has paper insert label.

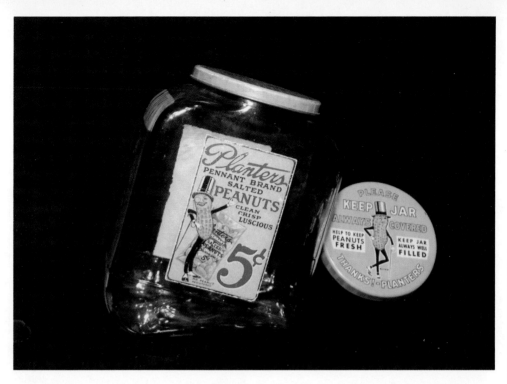

Streamline label, glass peanut jar, Pennant brand with a vertical rectangle. 1937. $175-275.

Streamline glass jar with Planters Jumbo Block, paper label and tin lid. 1937. $100-200.

Glass jar with paper label for Planters Jumbo Block and a tin lid. 1937. $100-200.

Two versions of a streamline glass jar with paper label and tin lids. 1937. $100-200.

21

Streamline peanut jar. Modified version. Slants back with yellow letters. This jar has a tin lid. 1937. $60-90. More if it has cardboard insert or round insert labels.

Glass Clipper Jar in original box. 1938. 36-5 cent bags of salted peanuts. $300-350.

Clipper glass peanut jar with cardboard die cut of pretty girl and a tin lid. 1938. $100-200.

Clipper peanut jar. Slanted with embossed "Planters" from upper left to lower right. Has tin lid. 8.25". 1938. $60-90. More if it has paper insert label.

Anchor Hocking peanut jar. White frosted and red. Lists five product items. 1960. 7.625" without the lid. 7" diameter. $125-150.

Nickel peanut bag jar. Either a green tin lid or a baked-on red tin lid can be correct. 1940. $50-90.

Leap year peanut jar with "Planters" embossed from upper left corner to lower right corner, on the front. Tin lid. 1940. $60-90.

Three glass peanut butter jars. 1950s.
$50-80 each.

Glass jar with green paper label. The lid
was anodized gold. It had to be punc-
tured to release the pressure in order to
open it. Late 1930s. $50-80.

Red lid nut jars with green labels. 1940s. $35-45 each.

Glass peanut butter jars with variations in size and labels. 1940s. $20-30.

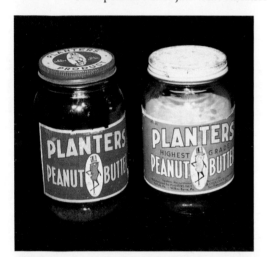

Glass peanut butter jars with two variations of labels. 1940s. $20-35.

Planters glass jars with a variety of sizes and nuts. 1940s. $20-30.

One pint of peanut oil in glass jar. 1930s. $50-75.

Drinking glass with yellow Mr. Peanut design. 1959. $15-20.

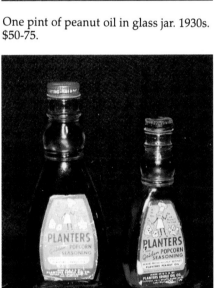

Two popcorn oil bottles. 1950s. $50-80 each.

Glass mug with yellow fired-on design. 1959. $15-20.

Mr. Peanut on drinking glass. 1950s.
$125-150.

Two versions of the circus
drinking glasses. Each has
a different design. 1950s.
5.5". $100-125.

Stem cocktail glasses with Mr. Peanut
standing upright, holding up the U- and
the V-shaped bowls. 1940s. The U-shape
glass $200-300. The V-shaped glass $500
and up.

Glass commemorating the opening of a new plant in San Francisco. 1954. Very rare piece. Price not available.

Souvenir glass brandy snifter with imprinted gold overlay of a variety of products. 9.25" tall. 1960s. $100-150.

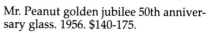

Ceramic cup with rhinestone in monocle. 1950s. 4". $200-300.

Mr. Peanut golden jubilee 50th anniversary glass. 1956. $140-175.

Set of Mr. Peanut china. $95-125 each piece. 1930s-40s.

Ceramic salt and pepper set. Has rhinestone in left monocle. 5". 1958. $60-90.

Ceramic handle salad set with wooden fork and spoon. Has rhinestone in left eye monocle. 9.875". 1958. $85-125.

Ceramic oil and vinegar set. 7.5". 1958.
$100-150.

Salt and pepper shakers with vinegar
and oil cruets in metal rack. Cork lined
stoppers on cruet set. 1948, 5.5". $300-
400.

Ceramic pitcher and cups. Green pants on Mr. Peanut. "Miyata Ware" and "Made in
Japan" on bottom. 1930s. $500 and up for the pitcher. $300 and up for the cup.

Ceramic ashtrays. 4.25". Left: has 3 peanuts on the back. Made in Japan. 1930s. $60-90. Right: has 2 peanuts on the back plus other slight differences. Rarer. Made in Japan. 1950s. $100-175.

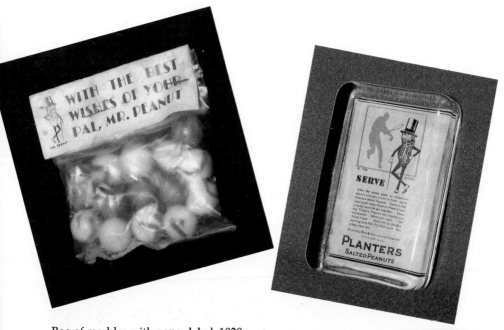

Bag of marbles with paper label. 1930s. $10-20. A reproduction was made in a net bag.

Glass paperweight with tennis player design. 1938. 4.25" x 2.75" x 1". $40-70.

Jewelry

Charm bracelet with 6 plastic charms. 1941. $15-25.

Metal employee badges with Planters logo on the right buckle, 1930s, and Planters on the left, 1950s. Price not available.

Lucky Mr. Peanut World Fair pins. 1.75". 1940s. $55-75 each.

Wooden Mr. Peanut pin. 1.75". 1940s. $40-50.

Mr. Peanut Santa pin. 1.75". 1940s. $100-200.

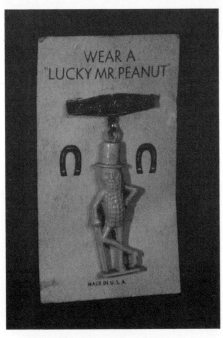

Souvenir plastic "Lucky Mr. Peanut." 2.75". 1940s. $40-50.

Mr Peanut pin with red rhinestone eye and green rhinestones on body. 1940s. $50-75.

Cameo ring (adjustable). 1950s. $25-35.

One and two year safety award pins from the company. 1950s. $30-40 each.

Metal old-style Mr. Peanut service pins. 10 year, 15 year, 20 year and 25 year with diamond chip. $50-100 each. Pre-1961.

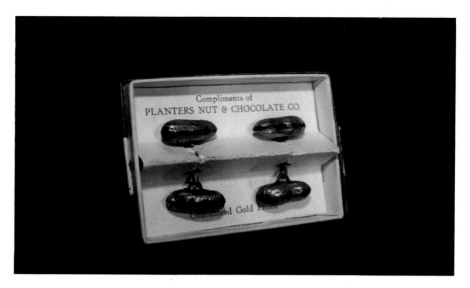

Gold wash peanut-shaped cuff links. 5". 1950s. $60-90.

Victory pins. Tip top with plastic Mr. Peanut on either large or small size. Each has curly-Q top ring. 1944. $25-35.

Metal and Tin

Suffolk brand salted peanuts, 10 pound tin. 1915-1918. Price not available.

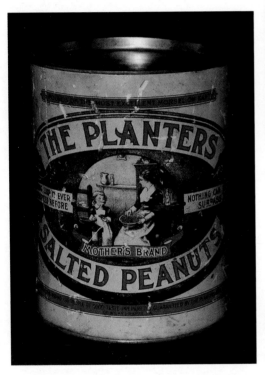

The Planters Salted Peanuts. "Mother's Brand." 5 pound tin. 1906-1910. Price not available.

The Planters Clean Crisp salted 10 pound peanuts tin. 1915-1918. $600 and up.

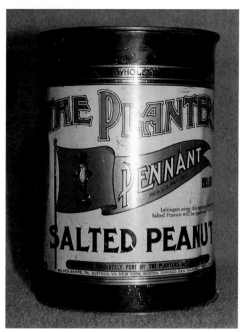

Planters tin with paper label. Held 10 pounds of Nutola Brand peanuts. 1920s. Price not available.

Ten pound tin has Mr. Peanut on left side of red Pennant. 1920s. $40-80.

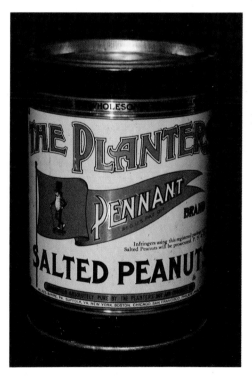

Sal-in-Shell Peanuts tin. 10 pound. 1930s-1940s. $500-and up.

The Planters salted peanuts "Pennant Brand", 5 pound tin. 1930s. $80-125.

Ten pound tin with lid that caps over the rim. Sign on the left side of the red pennant. 1909. $55-100.

Ten pound tin with Mr. Peanut on left side of red Pennant. Red band around top of tin states it contains 5 Jumbo Block Peanut Candy free in the can. 1920s. $45-80.

Ten pound tin with lid that fits inside rim. Hanging sign on the left side of the red pennant. 1909. $55-100.

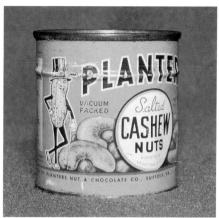

Planters salted peanut two ounce pocket tin. Rare. 1923. Price not available.

4 ounce cashew tin, unopened. 1940s. $40-50. Empty $20-25.

6 3/4 oz. cashew tin. 1940s. $15-25.

4 oz. Cocktail Peanut tin. 1938. $15-25.

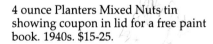

4 ounce Planters Mixed Nuts tin showing coupon in lid for a free paint book. 1940s. $15-25.

3 piece gift pack of 8 ounce nut tins. 1944. $150-250.

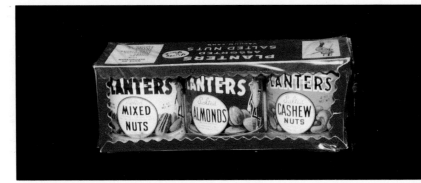

3 piece gift pack of 4 ounce nut tins. 1944. $150-250.

4 piece gift pack of 4 ounce nut tins. 1944. $200-300.

3 piece gift pack of 3 ounce nut tins. 1940s-50s. $250-350.

3 piece gift pack of 4 ounce cocktail peanuts. 1940s-50s. $95-150.

3 oz. Salted Pecans tin. 1940s. $20-25.

8 oz. Cocktail Peanut tin. 1938. $5-8.

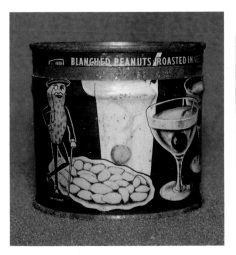

8 oz. Blanched Peanuts tin. 1940. $10-20.

One pound tin found in blue/green, light blue and darker blue. 1919. $80-120.

Egyptian nut tin with Planters Nut and Chocolate Co. written on inside of lid. 6.25" round. 1919. Rare. Price not available.

Planters Clean Crisp square salted nuts tin. One pound. 1915-1918. Price not available.

Square one pound tin of Planters Milk Chocolate Peanuts. 1919. Price not available.

42

Small nut tins. 1940s-50s. $15-25 each.

25 pound Bo-Lo Peanut Butter tin. 1930s. $250-300.

Peanut butter tin with handle. Has yellow, black and red lettering. 16 ounces. 1910-1918. Price not available.

Peanut butter tin with handle and paper label. 1920s. $750 and up.

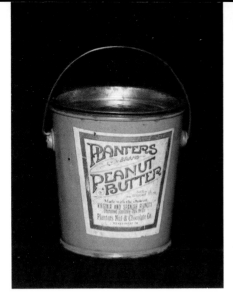

Planters tin pail of peanut butter. 16 ounces. 1930s. Price not available.

Tin for 80 pounds of peanut butter, with paper label. 1930s-1940s. $300 and up.

Tin bucket of Standard Peanut Butter. 25 pounds. 1918. 250-500.

Planters one pound High Grade Peanut Butter. 1918. Rare. Price not available.

Tin peanut butter bucket. 25 pounds. 1914. Rare. Price not available.

Canadian peanut butter tins. 1940s. $75-125.

Tin 10 pound bucket of Planters peanut butter. 1914. Price not available.

Tin pail of High Grade Peanut Butter. 5 pounds. 1918. Rare. Price not available.

One half pint of Ali D'Italia peanut oil. 1930s. $100-200.

One gallon peanut oil Ali D'Italia. 1930s. Price not available.

One pint of Hi-Hat peanut oil. 1930s. $50-75.

High Grade Peanut Butter tin. 25 pounds. 1918. $250-500.

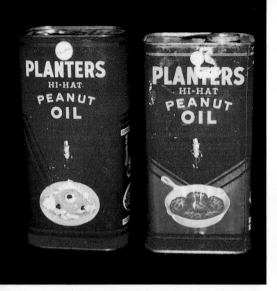

Quart of Hi-Hat peanut oil. The version on the right is Canadian with French writing. 1930s. $50-100.

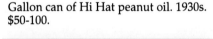
One half gallon can of Hi Hat peanut oil. 1930s. $50-100.

Gallon can of Hi Hat peanut oil. 1930s. $50-100.

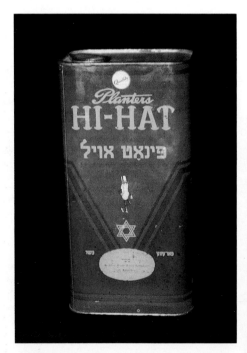

One half gallon can of Hi-Hat peanut oil with Hebrew writing and star of David. 1930s. $150-200.

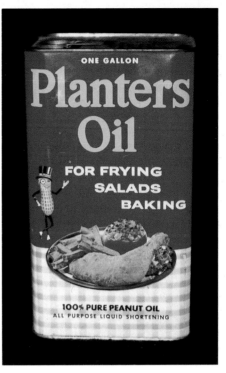

Planters Novola Peanut Oil from Canada. 37.5 pounds. 1950s. $60-100.

One gallon Planters oil. 1950s. $30-50.

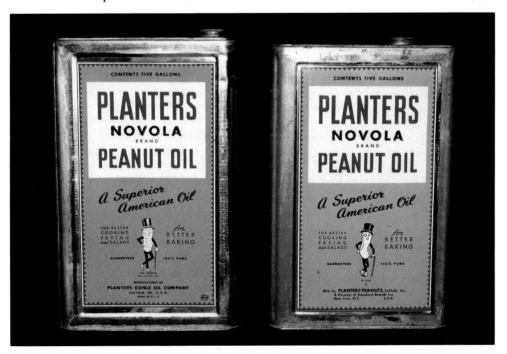

Two 5 gallon Novola Peanut Oil tins with different graphics. 1950s. $60-100.

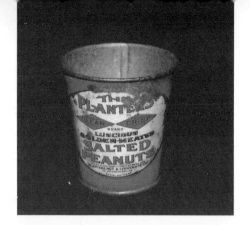

Tin cup for measuring peanuts from a larger container. 2.5". 1909. Rare. Price over $300.

Pennant brand tin nut measuring scoop. 2.75". Held 1.45 ounces of peanuts. Can have some color variations. 1924. $75-125.

Enamel Mr. Peanut display sign from Memphis, Tennessee. 78" x 32.5". 1948. Price not available.

Plexiglass display sign. "Planters Nut Department". 26" x 10". 1950s. $60-100

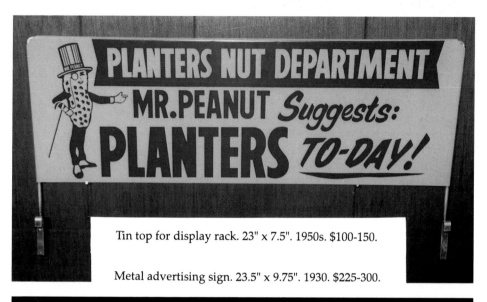

Tin top for display rack. 23" x 7.5". 1950s. $100-150.

Metal advertising sign. 23.5" x 9.75". 1930. $225-300.

Tin display rack for peanut specialties. 14" x 4". 1930s. Price not available.

Tin 5 cent Jumbo Peanut Block display. 12". 1930s. Price not available.

Enamel 10 cent peanut wall vending machine. 1940s. $500 and up.

Tin nut dishes in wartime victory box. 1940s. $35 dish, $45 for the box.

1940 World's Fair tin nut dishes. One large and four individual small dishes. $30-45.

Common tin nut dish set. One large and four small individual dishes. 1930s-40s. $8-15.

1939 World's fair tin nut dishes. One large and four individual small dishes. 1939. $20-30.

Metal green Lincoln toy truck with advertising sign on side. 13.5". Also made in red. Rare. 1940s. Price not available.

Metal nut chopper. Fits on top of a can of nuts. 1950s. $15-20. Original mailing box adds to price. $20-35.

Greeting coaster. Metal, 1955. Three different styles not shown. $3-5.

Tin lighter shaped like the cocktail peanut can. 1.5". 1940s. $70-100.

Letter openers. Bottom: two peanut handle, 1920s. Price not available. Middle: 1929. 8.5". Price not available. Top: large peanut handle, 1950s. Price not available.

Metal peanut-shaped lighter with original box. 2.5". 1930s. $70-100.

Pot metal statue of Mr. Peanut. 7". 1930s. $500-600.

Metal chocolate candy mold of full figure Mr. Peanut. 8.25" tall. 1955. $300-400.

Left: ashtray marked 50th anniversary at back of feet. 1956. $25-35; Middle: plain gold wash Mr. Peanut ashtray. 1970s. $15-20; Right: chrome Mr. Peanut. 1992. $35-55.

Left: Aluminum deep fryer with only one Mr. Peanut on the side. Has thermometer hanging on the side. $50-75; Middle: Funnel set with all six pieces, 1934. $200; Right: 3 Mr. Peanuts on side with basket insert. $50-75.

Gold wash and silver plate, nut serving spoon. 1940s-50s. $10-15 each.

Pair of copper peanut roaster decorations. 1920s-30s. $200-300.

Silver plated baby cup with Mr. Peanut engraved on front. 2.5" x 2.375". 1950s. $75-90.

Paper and Cardboard

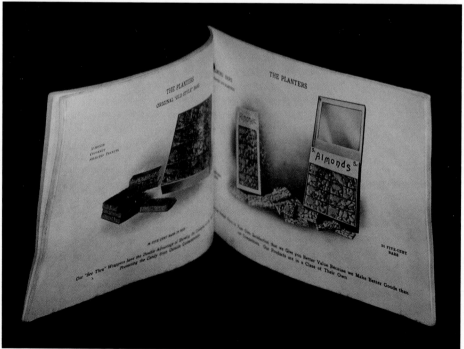

Planters, "See-Thru Package," book. Front and inside. 5" x 10". 1910-1919 era. Rare. Price not available.

Paper invoices from the 1920s. $10-20 each.

Employee's paper hat with Mr. Peanut in the corner and a nut in upper corner. 1950s. $20-30.

Cardboard box for 5 cent packages. Circa 1930. rare. Price not available.

Cardboard box for 5 cent Coco Peanut Bars. Circa 1930. Rare. $75-125.

Large cardboard shipping box for Clean Crisp Peanut Bars. 1940s. $75-125.

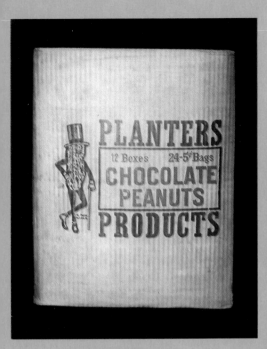

Planters 5 cent Chocolate Peanuts cardboard shipping box. 1940s. Price not available.

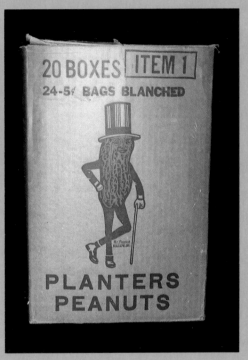

Twenty boxes of twenty four 5 cent bags of blanched peanuts, cardboard shipping box. 1930s. $100-150.

Cardboard 5 cent Chocolate Peanuts bag container. Circa 1930. Rare. Price not available.

Cardboard die cut advertising with original 5 cent glassine bags of peanuts and the original cardboard shipping box. 1920s. Rare. Price not available.

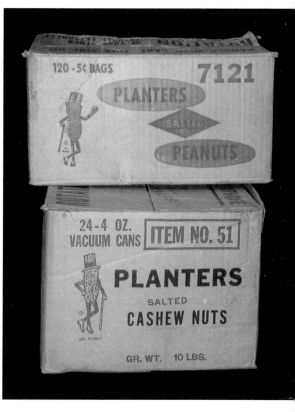

Planters Penny Lunch Peanut Bars
cardboard shipping box. 1920s. Rare.
Price not available.

Cardboard 5 cent shipping box for
Planters Salted Peanuts and cashews. 10
pounds. 1950s. Rare. Price not available.

Cardboard peanut boxes from 1916-
1918. Rare. Prices not available.

Cardboard box and sleeve for 5 cent Peanut Butter Sandwiches. 1950s. Rare. Price not available.

Cardboard shipping boxes. Bottom one for 10 cent bags of peanuts, and top one for twenty-four 4 ounce vacuum cans of chopped peanuts. 1950s. $25-50. 093/s14

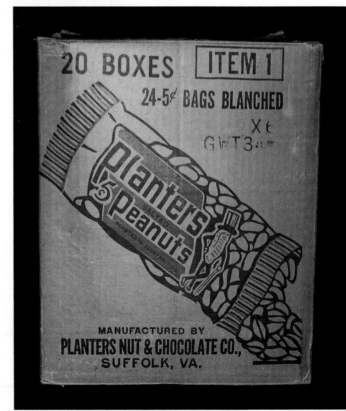

Planters 5 cent bag of nuts shipping box. 1950s. $75-125.

Eight Planters circus cardboard boxes for 5 cent bars. 1920s. Rare. Price not available.

Cardboard die cut box and sleeve for 5 cent Salted Peanuts bags. 1940s. Rare. Price not available.

Two boxes for peanuts. 1940s. Boxes replaced cans during war effort. Price not available.

Two inner and outer boxes for the Salted Peanut bags. Airplane die cut. 1944. Rare. Price not available.

Cardboard sleeve and die cut box for the 5 cent peanut bags. "Pick of the Plantation". 1940s. Rare. Price not available.

Cardboard box for Planters 5 cent peanuts. The front of the box shows black and white people picking peanuts in the field. Circa 1928. Rare. Price not available.

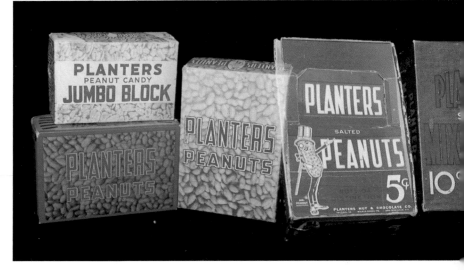

Several boxes for 5 and 10 cent bags of peanuts. 1945. Rare. Price not available.

Cardboard box for 5 cent Salted Peanuts. Circa 1928. Rare. Price not available.

Two cardboard peanut boxes with sleeves for the 5 cent peanut butter sandwiches. 1945. Rare. Price not available.

Cardboard box and sleeve for 5 cent bags of peanuts. 1944. Rare. Price not available.

Cardboard box and sleeve for 5 cent bags of peanuts. 1940s. Rare. Price not available.

Cardboard boxes and sleeves for 5 cent bags of peanuts. 1948. Rare. Price not available.

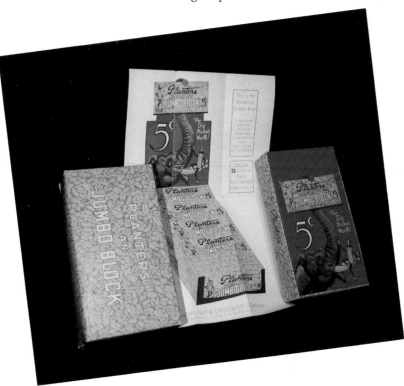

Cardboard die cut and box with sleeve for 5 cent Jumbo Block. 1940s. Rare. Price not available.

Cardboard peanut box for 5 cent Sugared Peanuts, single serve size. 1930s. Rare. Price not available.

Cardboard boxes and sleeve for the 1 cent bag of nuts. 1920s. Box on the right was waxed. Rare. Price not available.

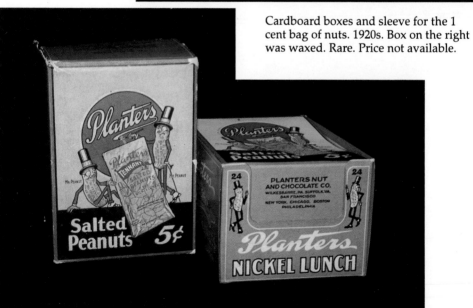

Cardboard box for the 5 cent Planters nickel lunch. 1929. Rare. Price not available.

Cardboard peanut boxes. 1920s. Rare.
Prices not available.

Cardboard box for the 5 cent Salted
Peanut bags. Circa 1930s. Rare. Price not
available.

Cardboard box for the 5 cent Jumbo
Peanut Blocks. Circa 1930s. Rare. Price
not available.

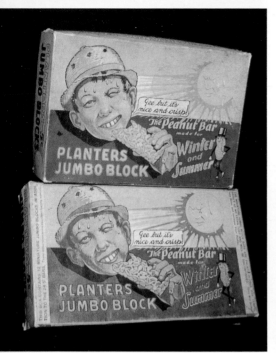

Two variations Planters Jumbo Block Peanut Bar containers. 1930s. Rare. Price not available.

Cardboard Candied Peanuts 5 cent box. Circa 1930s. Rare. Price not available.

Cardboard 5 cent chocolate-covered peanut bag container. "The world goes 'nuts'". Circa 1930. Rare. Price not available.

Original paper label from Planters Old Fashioned candy. 11.5" x 5". 1938. Rare. Price not available.

Cardboard box and sleeve for the 1 cent bag of peanuts. 1930s. Rare. Price not available.

Laminated candy bar wrappers. Jumbo Block peanut bar and Milk Chocolate Peanut Brittle Wafer. 1919. Rare. No price available.

Salesman's sample of Old Fashioned Jumbo Block candy bar. Bent over Mr. Peanut in the corner. 1959. $75-100.

Wax paper liner for candy box with Mr. Peanut logo. 1940s. $3-5.

Three varieties of Jumbo Block candy bar wrappers. 1950s-60s. $4-8.

Glassine and cellophane peanut bags. 1928-40. $15-25.

Glassine peanut bags. 1950s Pennant bags, $5-8. 1920s bags-$20-25.

Paper store peanut bags. 1950s. $5-15 each.

Glassine peanut bags. 1940s. $8-15 each.

Glassine 5 cent peanut bags. 1945-50. $8-12.

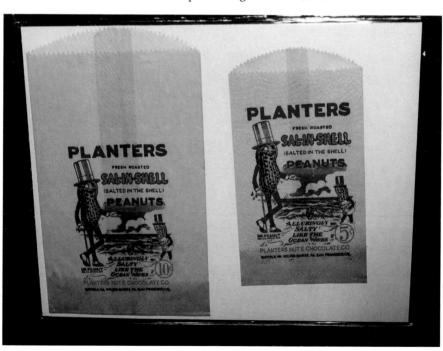

"Sal-in-Shell" glassine peanut bags. 1940s. $10-20.

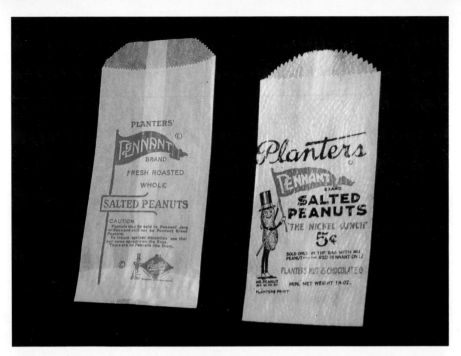

Glassine nickel bags. Two of many designs. 1920s- 30s. $6-10.

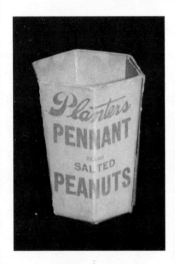

Waxed cardboard cup to measure out the peanuts. 2.5". 1920s. Rare. Price not available.

Large brown paper shopping bag with Mr. Peanut printed on front. 1950s. $10-20.

Small brown paper shopping bag with Mr. Peanut printed on front. 1950s. $10-20.

Cardboard cone scoop, holder for peanuts. 9". Circa 1929. Rare. Price not available.

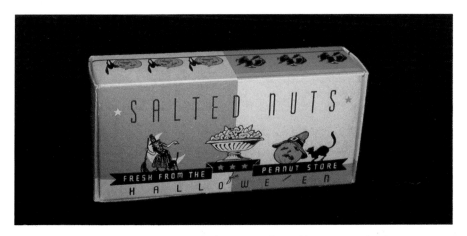

Halloween one pound Salted Nuts cardboard box. 1950s. $30-50.

Stripped greeting box from Planters, with Mr. Peanut logo. 1940s. $50-70.

Three boxes for Planters chocolate candy. Circa 1940s. Rare. Price not available.

Cardboard die cut blotters with Cocktail Peanuts and peanut butter jar, both in a peanut shape. 1940s. $40-50 each.

Cardboard die cut blotters with Cocktail Peanuts and a spilled bag of peanuts, both in a peanut shape. 1940s-50s. $40-50 each.

Cardboard die cut blotter with Hi Hat oil, advertising in a peanut shape. 1940s-50s. $40-50.

Peanut shaped die cut cardboard ink blotters. 1940s. $30-50 each.

Paper ad for charm bracelet. 1940s. $20-30.

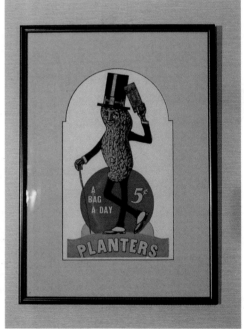

Framed die cut Mr. Peanut. He has
peanuts for fingers. 13". 1930s. $250-350.

Framed advertising with paint book.
1949. $35-45.

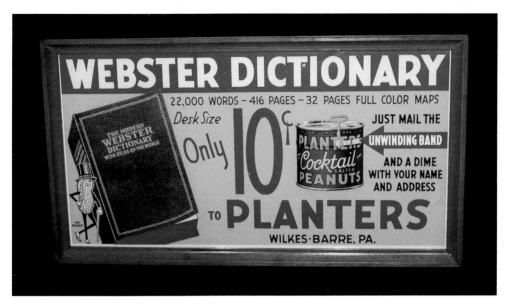

Trolley advertising sign for Webster's dictionary. 11" x 21". 1940s-50s. $200-275.

Framed Canadian picture. 1940s. $300-400.

A field of Peanuts in Sunny Virginia. The seeds are the Kernels Planted in May. The matured Peanuts are Harvested in October.

①

A WARM SANDY SOIL IS NEEDED FOR PROPER DEVELOPMENT

THIS

PEANUTS (ARACHIS HYPOGEA) Do not Grow On Trees. They Grow and Mature under Ground.

In October, when matu Laborers follow the pl the soil from the vines

②

THIS SHOWS THE

Set of 5 pictures showing how peanuts were grown. 1940s. Price not available.

After plowing, the Plants are stacked in the field around poles to dry in the wind and Sun. Peanuts are soft and damp when first plowed up . . . . .

③

THE PEANUT PLANTS ARE LEFT IN THESE "SHOCKS" UNTIL SUFFICIENTLY DRIED.

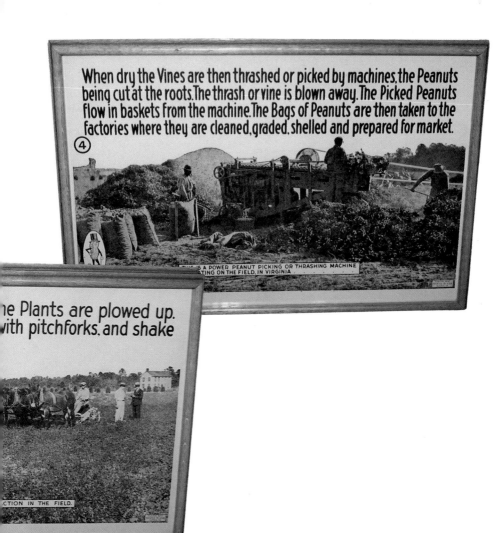

When dry the Vines are then thrashed or picked by machines, the Peanuts being cut at the roots. The thrash or vine is blown away. The Picked Peanuts flow in baskets from the machine. The Bags of Peanuts are then taken to the factories where they are cleaned, graded, shelled and prepared for market.

④

THIS IS A POWER PEANUT PICKING OR THRASHING MACHINE ...ATING ON THE FIELD, IN VIRGINIA.

...e Plants are plowed up. ...ith pitchforks, and shake

...CTION IN THE FIELD.

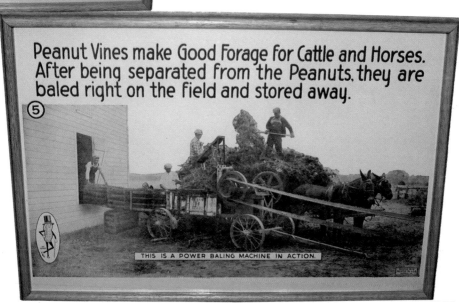

Peanut Vines make Good Forage for Cattle and Horses. After being separated from the Peanuts, they are baled right on the field and stored away.

⑤

THIS IS A POWER BALING MACHINE IN ACTION.

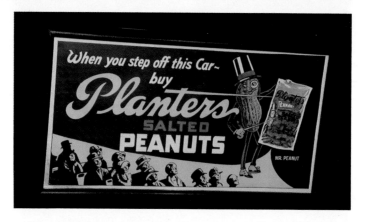

Framed advertising sign for trolley cars. 11" x 21". 1930s. $200-250.

Framed advertising sign for trolley cars. 11" x 21". 1930s. $200-250.

Framed Canadian, advertising sign for trolley cars. 10" x 21". 1930s. $200- 275.

Framed advertising trolley car sign. 11" x 21". 1930s. $200-250.

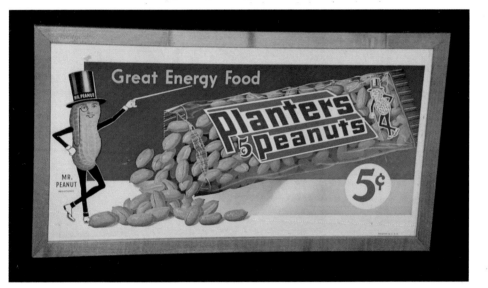

Framed advertising trolley car sign. 11" x 21". 1930s. $200-250.

Framed advertising trolley car sign. 11" x 21". 1930s. $200-250.

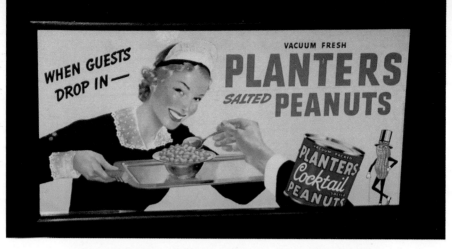

Framed advertising trolley car sign. 11" x 21". 1930s. $200-250.

Centerfold ad from *Saturday Evening Post*, 1936. This ad was in error, as it was the company's 30th and Mr. Peanut's 20th anniversary. $20-30.

Vineyard Maid trolley sign. 1930s. 11" x 22". $150-200.

Framed centerfold from *Saturday Evening Post* magazine. 1931. $20-30.

Various post cards. 1940s-70s. $6-20.

Various post cards. 1940s-1970s. $6-20.

Various post cards from Atlantic City.
1940s. $5-15 each.

Various post cards from Atlantic City. 1940s. $5-15 each.

Various post cards from Atlantic City. 1950s. $6-15.

Various post cards from Atlantic City. 1940s-1950s. $5-20 each.

Four greeting cards from the Planters company. 1950s-60s. $15-20 each.

Cardboard header cards for pull tabs games. 1950s. $15-25 each.

Cardboard header cards for pull tab games. 1950s. $15-25 each.

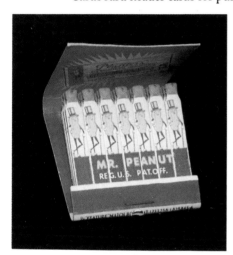

Book of Mr. Peanut matches. Mr. Peanut on each match. 1930s. $75-100.

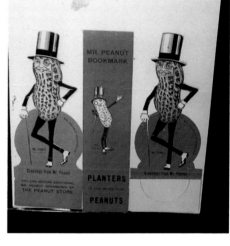

Three orange cardboard book marks. 1930s-40s. $15-20 each.

Yellow Mr. Peanut figure book marks. 1930s-40s. $15-20 each.

Original envelope with eight seed
packets and planting guide book. 1947.
$90-125.

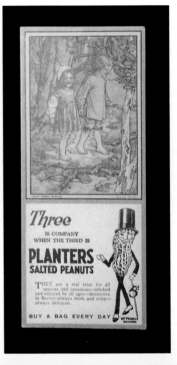

Cardboard ink blotter, "Babes in
Woods." 1920s. $50-75.

Double deck of playing cards with Mr. Peanut rowing the boat. 1932. $200-250.

Canadian animal trade cards set of 25. 4.25" x 3.5". 1940s. $100-150 set.

American set of 25 trade cards. 1.75" x 2.5". 1940s. $75-100 set.

Roll of trick or treat decorative paper. 1940. $8-12.

Free souvenir paper coupon. 1950s-60s. $10-15.

Free, souvenir paper coupon for Conventions and Visitors. 1950s-60s. $10-15.

Two spooky card versions. 1950s-60s. $3-6 each.

Paper, ad for "fascinating" premiums from Planters Peanuts. 1950s. $10-20.

Paper ad for silver baby cup. 1950s. 15-25.

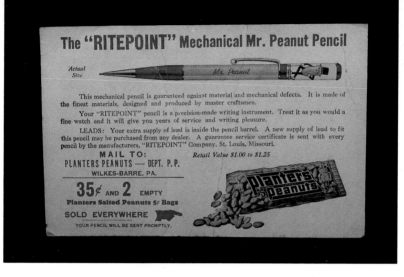

Paper ad for "Ritepoint" pencil with oil top. 1950s. $15-20.

Advertising card featuring Eddie Fisher on "Planters Peanut Time." Companion to the 45 rpm record. 1956. $30-40

Cardboard hand-held advertising fan with moving wheels. Both sides. 8" x 5.25". 1940s. $150-200.

Promotional record for Planters by Eddie Fisher. "Planters Peanut Time." Late 50s. $65-100.

Cardboard Planters megaphone. 1940s. $300-400.

Cardboard Planters advertising fan with moving wheels and wooden handle. Same picture on the front as previous fan. 8". 1940s. $200-300.

Cardboard child's suitcase with Mr. Peanut logo on front. 7.25" x 8". 1940s. $100-150.

Cardboard ring toss game with rubber rings. 1940s. $150-200.

Original envelope with balloon and cardboard feet, Mr. Peanut figure. 1940s-1950s. $100-150.

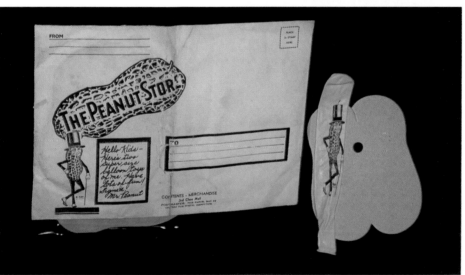

Cardboard score board from the 50s. $30-45.

Cardboard Mr. Peanut paint pallet set.
9" x 4.5". 1954. $45-65.

Paper pop gun with peanut advertising
on end and Mr. Peanut logo on handle.
8.5". 1940s. $200-300.

Planters Pioneers of the Santa Fe Trail,
game board in box. 1935. $80-125.

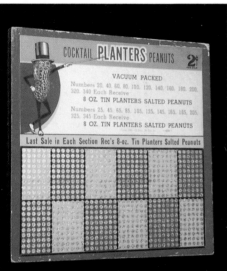

Original mailing envelope with Mr. Peanut jiggle face cardboard puzzle. Chain moves to make different faces. 1920s. $100-150.

Cardboard punchboard. 2 cents. 1930s-50s. $60-100.

Cardboard punchboards. 1 cent. 1930s-50s. $60-100.

Cardboard punchboards. 2 cents. 1930s-50s. $60-100.

Cardboard punchboard. 5 cent. 1930s-50s. $60-100.

Cardboard 2 cent punchboard. 1930s-40s. $50-100.

Cardboard 3 cent punchboard. Not uncommon. 1938. $100-150.

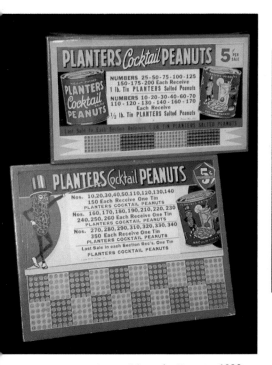

Cardboard punchboards. 5 cents. 1930s-50s. $60-100.

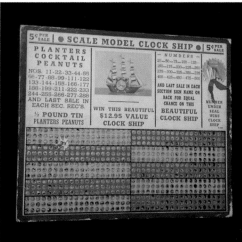

Cardboard punchboard. 5 cents. 1930s-50s. $60-100.

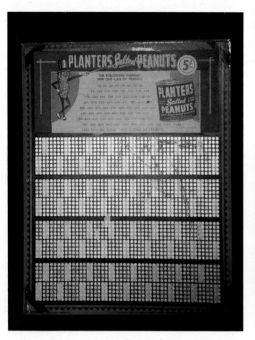

Cardboard 5 cent punchboard. 1940s.
$50-75.

Cardboard pull tab game. One cent
header on non-refillable stand. 1940s-
60s. $100-125.

Cardboard 10 cent pull tab game on
wooden non-refillable stand. 1940s-60s.
$80-110.

Planters 5 cent cardboard punchboard.
1930s. In unused condition. $40-60.

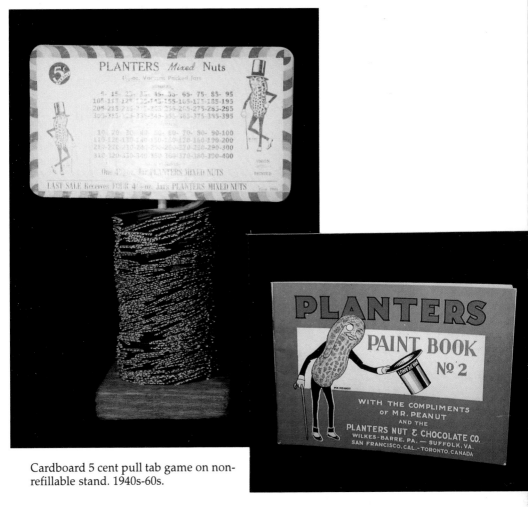

Cardboard 5 cent pull tab game on non-refillable stand. 1940s-60s.

Planters Paint Book No. 2. 28 pages. 1929. $20-35.

Story books, "Dedicated to the Children..." 1928. Left: Canada. Right: America. $30-50.

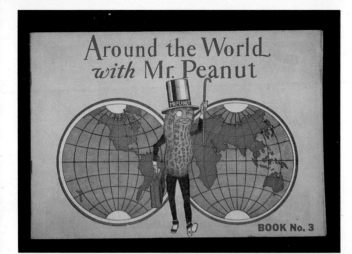

Around the World with Mr. Peanut story book. 28 pages 1930. $20-35.

Famous Men story and paint book with 28 pages. 1935. $20-35.

The United States of America historical and educational paint book. 1949. $15-25.

Planters Jolly Time Paint Book. 1947. $12-25.

The Making of America, story and paint book. 28 pages. 1938. $20-35.

Seeing the U.S.A. educational paint book. 1950. $20-30.

Planters Happy Time Paint Book. 1946. $12-25.

The Colorful Story of Peanuts as told by Mr. Peanut. 1957. $15-25.

Presidents of the United States story book. Through Hoover. 1932. $20-30.

Presidents of the United States of America, two versions, Washington through Eisenhower, paint book. 1950s. $15-25.

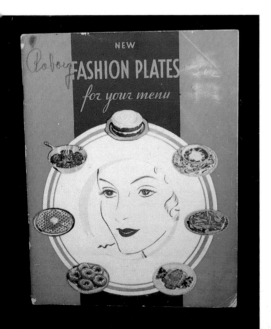

Fashion Plates for Your Menu cook book from Planters. 1932. $10-15.

Booklet from Hi Hat peanut oil,
Planters. 1940s-50s. $10-15.

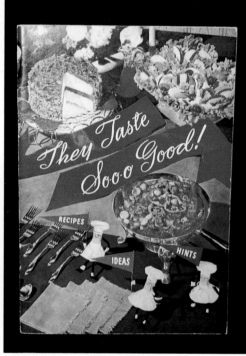

They Taste Sooo Good, cook book from
Planters. 1940s. $8-15.

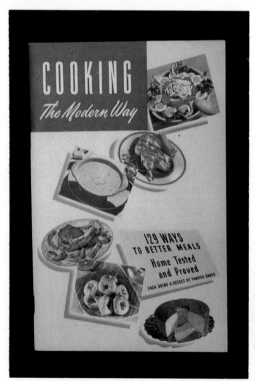

Cooking the Modern Way cook book from
Planters. 1948. $8-15.

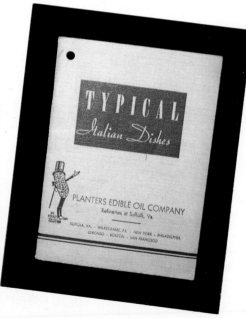

Typical Italian Dishes cook book from
Planters. 1940s. $10-20.

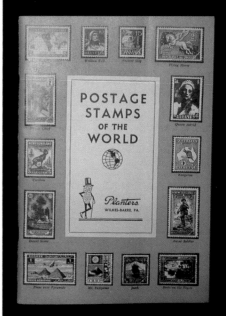

Postage Stamps of the World book. 9" x 6.5". 1940s. $15-65.

The Sportsman's Cook Book on Fish and Seafood Cookery from Planters. 1942. $10-20.

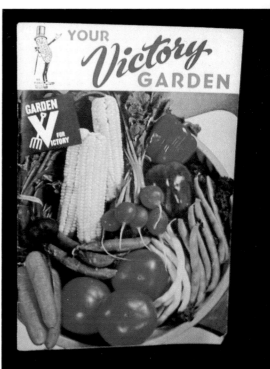

Booklet "Helping the Veteran Help Himself" from Planters. 1944. $25-45.

Your Victory Garden booklet from Planters. 1945. $15-25.

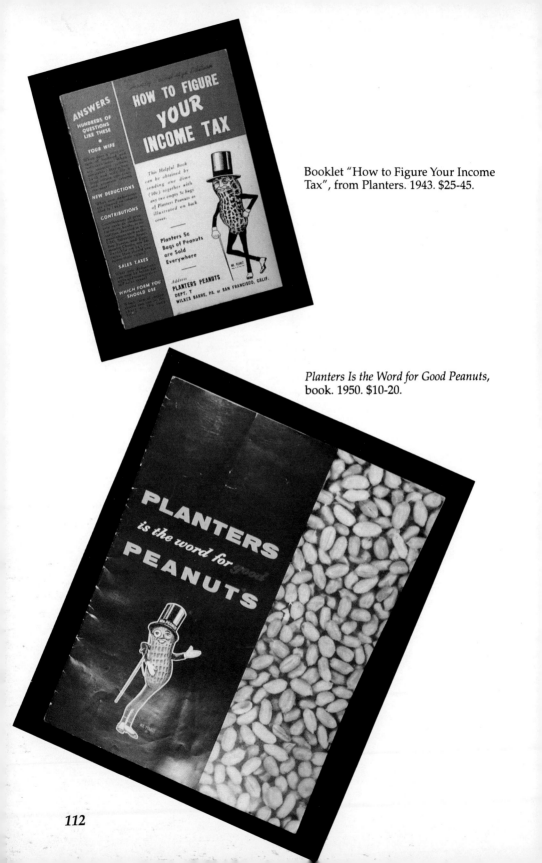

Booklet "How to Figure Your Income Tax", from Planters. 1943. $25-45.

Planters Is the Word for Good Peanuts, book. 1950. $10-20.

Plastic

Plastic key thermometers with Mr. Peanut pin in center of top. 8.5". 1940s. $50-75.

Plastic figural Mr. Peanut electric lamps. 9.75". 1950s. $200-300 each.

Plastic doilies in cellophane package. Came as a set of 4 in yellow, pink or white. 1959. $15-25.

Plastic cookie cutters. Two different styles of Mr. peanut. Red translucent on original cardboard. 1950s. $15-25.

Plastic cookie cutters. Two different styles of Mr. Peanut. Blue translucent on original yellow cardboard. 1950s. $15-25.

Plastic food pick and fork. Mr. Peanut sitting on tops. 1950s. $1-2 each.

Peanut-shaped footed nut dishes. Plastic with Mr. Peanut in bottom of dish. 4". 1960s. $6-10.

Bent leg Mr. Peanut salt and pepper shakers. Came in tan, green, red, light blue, yellow, white, orange, pink, silver and gold. $5-8. 1950s. If "Made in Canada" on bottom $10-20.

Table salt and pepper shakers. Plastic mug with a snap on lid also comes in a variety of colors and different color lids. 1950s. 5". $10-15.

Plastic straight leg salt and pepper sets. Red, tan, green, light blue, pink, orange, gold, black/tan. 1950s. 4". $8-15.

Plastic cocktail glasses. 1950s. 5.125".
Red, green, blue and amber in both clear
and opaque. Also in translucent, red
clear, blue. $20-30.

Plastic cocktail/drink stirrers. 1950s. $4-8 each.

Plastic drink stirrers. 1950s. $3-5 each.

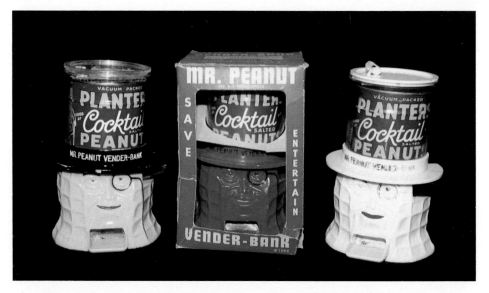

Three plastic Mr. Peanut Vender-Banks. A can of nuts sits in the hat. Nuts are dispensed through the neck area. 1950s. $150-250.

Four plastic compartmented nut dishes with standing Mr. Peanut in center. Tan, green, red, light blue. 1950s. $25-40.

Two plastic compartmented nut dishes with standing Mr. Peanut in center. 1950s. Green with white Mr. Peanut in center: $50-60: fluorescent: $75-100.

Clear plastic measuring cup. 4". 1950s. $6-12.

Plastic pink fluorescent cup. 1950s. $25-35.

Plastic cups. 4". 1950s. Tan, red, green, light blue, common colors, $5-9. Dark blue: $35-45; lime green: $55-70; pink: $25-40; yellow: $20-30.

Plastic stirrers and holders. 8.5". 1950s. $50-85 set. Came in red, tan, green and light blue.

Plastic peanut butter spreaders. 7". Red, tan, green, light blue and dark blue. Do not confuse them with the peanut butter spreaders (either yellow or red) that came with the peanut butter makers. 1950s. $4-8 each.

Plastic nut serving spoons. Red, tan, light blue and green. 1950s. $5-8 each.

Plastic measuring spoons. 1/4 teaspoon to 1 tablespoon. 1950s. $5-8 each.

Plastic baby rattles with a pair of plastic Mr. Peanut figures on the side of each rattle. 4.75". 1950s. $100-150 each.

Light weight plastic Mr. Peanut mask with top hat. 1950s. $125-175.

Santa Mr. Peanut, face mask. Thin plastic. 1950s. $125-175.

Plastic "Express Truck" and "Peanut Wagon." 5". 1960s. $250-350.

Plastic kazoo. 1950-60s. 4.75". $6-15. Also a reproduction version with a different shade of blue and Towana Kazoo Co. printed on ring.

Plastic Mr. Peanut kite, framed.
1950s. Price not available.

Plastic truck with carousal on back.
1950s. $250-350.

Plastic Mr. Peanut, peanut-shaped racing cars. 5.25". 1950s-60s. $250-350.

Hard rubber Jet Racers in original box. 1950s-60s. $250-350.

Plastic truck and stake trailer. 5.5". 1950s. $200-250 each.

Plastic Mr. Peanut with his vendor push cart, with original box. 6.5". 1950s. $200-250.

Gold and bronze tone Mr. Peanut plastic figural whistles. 1950s. $15-25 each.

Plastic Christmas ornaments which were also whistles. Solid colors and two tone colors. 3.5". 1950s. $20-25.

Plastic figural Mr. Peanut whistles. Came in red, green, tan, light blue, yellow, pink and tan/white. 1950s. $3-6 each.

Plastic Mr. Peanut banks. 9". 1950s. Tan, red, green, light colors. Old style: $10-15 each. New style: $5-8 each.

Plastic Mr. Peanut banks. 9". 1950s. Glow in the dark: $50-70; pink: $25-35; orange, $100-125.

Plastic Mr. Peanut banks. 1950s. 9".
Clear or black/tan: $40-60; light blue:
$5-10.

Plastic Mr. Peanut banks. 9". 1950s. Yellow: $20-30; lime green: $100-125; tan: $5-10.

Plastic walking Mr. Peanut, in
original box. 1950s-60s. $250-350.

Plastic with gold or silver wash Mr.
Peanut figural bank. 1950s. Very
rare. Price not available. Watch for
reproductions.

Red plastic Mr. Peanut bank. 1950s.
10.5". Very rare. Price not available.

Two versions of the plastic Mr. Peanut figural banks. 1950s. Rare. Price not available.

Plastic Mr. Peanut figural banks 1950s. Rare. Price not available.

Wind-up walker. Came in red, tan, green, light blue, and black/tan. 8.5". 1950s. $200-350.

Plastic whistles. Mr. Peanut embossed on one side, Planters embossed on other side. 2". 1950s. $6-10 each.

Plastic two piece nut containers. Originally came with cardboard paint set and paint brush inside. Mr. Peanut is embossed in bottom of bowl. Came in red, tan, green, clear, light blue, pink, yellow, clear white and two tone combinations. $8-12 without the paints, $40-50 with paints. 4". 1950s.

Plastic peanut party favors and lids with the paint sets and brush inside. 1950s. $40-60.

Child's plastic knife, fork and spoon set in red, light blue, green and yellow. 1950s. $15-25 set.

Two of the six versions of red and white oil top pens with Mr. Peanut in oil. $10-20. Also came with blue and orange with Mr. Peanut in oil. Rare. 1950s. $30 and up.

Mechanical black and gold pencils. Two versions. 1957. $10-20 each.

Red plastic child's tooth brush in original wrapper. Full size Mr. Peanut on end. 5". 1950s. $75-100.

Mr. Peanut plastic key chain and flashlight combination. 1950s. 3". Price not available.

Two versions six red and white mechanical pencils. Shown, tan and red plastic Mr. Peanuts. 1950s. $10-25 each.

Planters key chains with charms as peanut cans, 0.25". 1940s-50s. $20-25.

Blue and white plastic marking pen. 1940s-50s. $15-25 each.

Box cutter from the 1950s. $9-15.

Plastic stick pins. 1". Red, brown,
yellow, blue, turquoise and green. 1950s.
$4-6 each.

Mr. Peanut plastic charms. 2". 1950s. $2-3 each.

Wood

Wooden, Clean Crisp Peanut Bars, 72 count, shipping box. 1915-1920. $75-100.

Wooden "peanut pickers" crate. 1920s. Rare. Price not available.

Wooden shipping crate for Clean-Crisp Peanut Bars. 1915-1925.

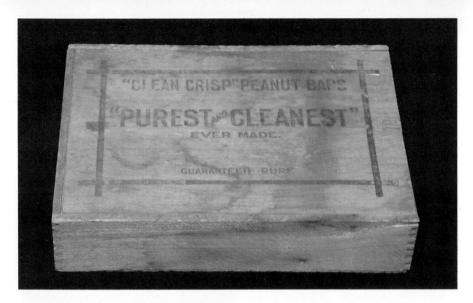

Wooden, Clean Crisp Peanut Bars, 72 count, shipping box. 1915-1920. $75-100.

Wooden, 1 cent Big bars, shipping box. 1915-1920. $75-100.

Clean Crisp Peanut Bar wooden box.
Held seventy-two 1 cent peanut bars.
7.5" x 11". 1920. $80-125.

Wooden shipping box for Planters Cluster bars. Rare. 1937. Price not available.

Wooden peanut butter shipping box. Held 12, 1 pound tins. 1920s. Price not available.

Hinged top wooden shipping crate. Held six 10-pound jars of Salted Peanuts. 1930s. $200-300.

Wooden shipping crate with the Clean Crisp logo. 1930. Price not available.

Wooden bucket that held 25 pounds of chocolate covered peanuts. 12.5" tall. 1930s. Price not available.

Wooden shipping crate with a red Mr. Peanut juggling red peanuts. 1940s. $150-250.

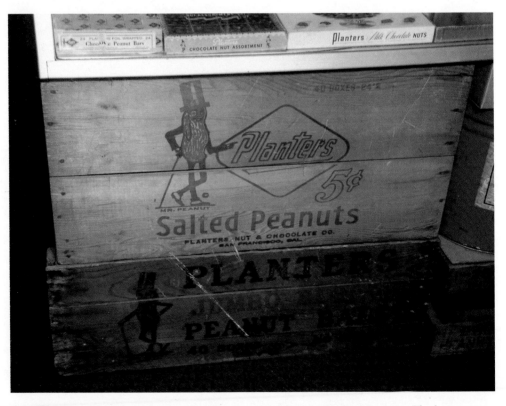

The top wooden box was for shipping 5-cent packages of Salted Peanuts. The bottom box held 40 boxes of Jumbo Block for shipping. 1930s. $225-275.

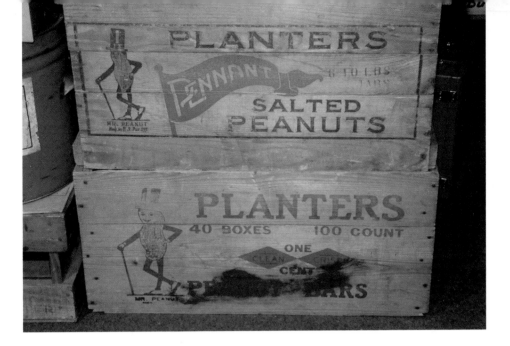

Top: wooden box for shipping six 10-pound peanut jars; bottom: shipping box for forty boxes of 100 count bags of peanuts. 1930s. $225-275.

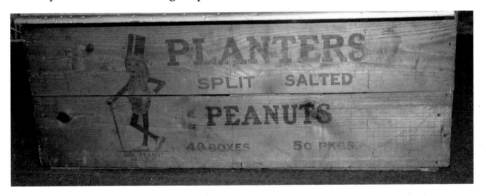

Wooden box for shipping forty boxes of 5 cent packages of peanuts. 1930s. $225-275.

Wooden shipping box for six 10-pound pails of peanut butter. 1930-1940. $225-275.

Three wooden shipping boxes. Top: six 10-pound cans, 1930s. $125-175; middle: 40 boxes, 1930s. $225-275; bottom: box for Nut Confections. 1920s-30s. $150-200.

Wooden jointed Mr. Peanut doll. Should have black wooden cane. 1930s. 9". $125-175.

Wooden shipping crate for the 1 cent Clean Crisp peanut bar. 1920s-30s. $250-350.

Wooden shipping crate for the "Nickel Lunch" peanut package. 1940s. $200-300.

Wood and plastic "whip it tops" from Planters, with original mailing package. 1947. $100-125 each.

Mr. Peanut wooden pencils. 2". 1950s. $20-30 set of seven.

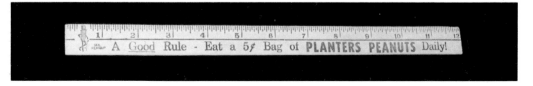

12 inch wooden ruler. 1940s. $20-30.

Miscellaneous

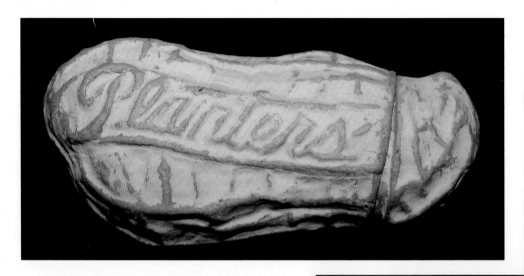

Papier mache peanut, end comes off to fill with a half-pound of peanuts. 1930s. $40-60.

Papier mache half-pound peanut containers. 12.5". The plain one is rarer. 1930s. $250-350.

Papier Mache peanut, end comes off to fill with one pound of peanuts. Shown with original box. 1930s. Nut: $35-60; box: $20-40.

Rubber hand puppet. Tan with black hat. 6.5". 1942. $750 and up.

Mr. Peanut rubber squeak toy. 1930s. Price not available.

Script metal 10 cent coin. Also came in 5 cent, 25 cent, 50 cent and $1 coins. 1920s. $80-120 each.

Metal child's knife, fork, and spoon set. Made by Charlton Silverplate. 1950s. $60-90 set.

New York felt pennant from 1939-40. Mr. Peanut in lights in background. $60-75.

Mr. Peanut in original plastic package. Cotton stuffed, cloth doll. 21". 1960. $12-20.

Various printers blocks. 1920s-1970s. $20-85. Watch for reproductions.

Camping set with Mr. Peanut paper sticker on each item. 1982. $20-30 set.

Cotton Mr. Peanut costume. 1930s-1940s. $150-200.

1959 salesman's sample kit. Price not available.

Reproductions

Cobalt blue cookie jar. Planters and Mr. Peanut embossed on front. 11.5". 1978. Reproduction barrel jar. $15-25. The reproduction is considerably smaller than the original barrel jar. It came in cobalt blue, clear, light green and opaque white ceramic with blue lettering.

White ceramic with blue detail reproduction of the octagonal peanut jar with blue peanut finial lid. Poor quality. 1978. $15-25.

Reproduction of the octagon (eight sided) peanut jars. Came in flame red (not shown), green, pink, clear, and cobalt blue. 12" with the peanut finial lid. 1980. $17-30. Around the collar of the reproduction jar the company name is spelled with the following bad spacing. PLANTE RS.

Fantasy version of the Barlow knife. 1980. $6-10 each.

Plastic advertising thimbles. Mr. Peanut logo on left thimble. "Planters Peanuts" on right thimble. Fantasy item. 1960s. $4-8 each.

Clear glass peanut jar with Pennant salted peanuts on front. 9" x 8" tall. Not authorized. "The everything jar," this reproduction combined three separate jars. Came in cobalt blue, clear and pink 1982. $17-30.

Four corner reproduction peanut jar. 1992. Came in pink, cobalt blue and clear. 11.75" without the peanut finial lid. $15-25. This jar is much heavier than the original.

Fantasy item. Mr. Peanut robot peanut jar. 1994. Came in pink, clear, dark green and cobalt blue. 11.75" with the peanut finial lid. $12-20.

Plastic coated advertising mirror. "The Nickel Lunch". 2" x 3". Authenticity questionable. 1970s. $5-8.

All reproduction knives. White or yellow. 1960s- 1980s. $2-6 each.

Real and reproduction jars. Left: Real with wide white space above the T's. and "Mr. Peanut" printed in white by his knees. 1937. $60-80. Right: Reproduction, narrow white above the T's and blue type by the knees. $20-25.

Plastic cigarette pack holder. 1970s. $8-15. Not authorized.

Cotton oven mitt with various trademarks including Mr. Peanut, shown as Mr. Nut. 1970s. $10-15.

Tin wall thermometer. 15.75" x 6". 1978. Fantasy item. $10-20.

Avon lipstick with the box. Plastic peanut. Not authorized. 1984. $3-5.

Display piece made of stuffed satin. Authenticity unknown. 1960s. Price unavailable.

Silk scarf with peanut design. Copy. 1970s. $3-5.

Two reproduction cast iron bottle openers. 1972. $40-60.

Miniature glass peanut jar filled with
seeds. Mr. Peanut logo painted on front.
1". Authenticity questionable. 1980s.
$12-18.

Ceramic full figure Mr. Peanut, salt and pepper set. "Taiwan". 4.25". 1989. Taiwan reproductions. $4-6.

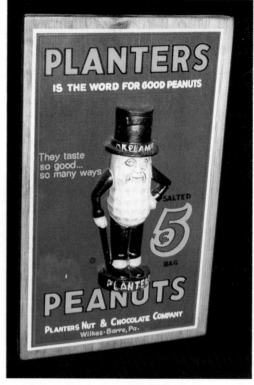

Paper wall plaque. (not authorized). 1980s. $15-30.

Ceramic spoon rest/wall hanger with nuts in the center signed "Cacahuates". 5.5" x 9". 1980s. $2-5. Not authorized.

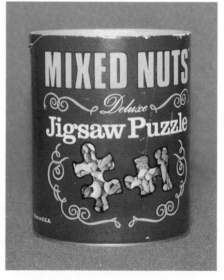

Jig saw puzzle by Synergistics, in a cardboard can that looks like a can of Planters mixed nuts. 1985. Fantasy item. $5-8.

Cast iron reproductions of Mr. Peanut door stops. 5.75", 7.975", 8.125", 11.25", 11.5". 1980s. $8-15 each.

Cobalt blue full figure glass, salt and pepper set. 6.75". 1994. $5-10. Fantasy item came in many colors.

Ceramic reproduction Mr. Peanut statue. 16.5". 1986. $50-60.

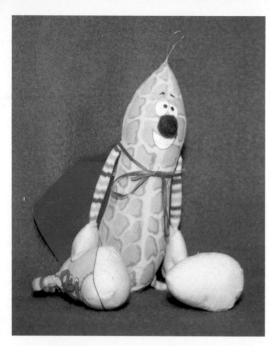

Cotton stuffed doll. 13". 1980s. $3-5. Not authentic.

Water cooler, origin unknown. Not authorized. 1989. Price unknown. Fantasy item.

Cash register. 2nd version with Mr. Peanut in center. Not authorized. Fantasy item. 1989. Price not available.

Plastic Mr. Peanut key chain. 3". Not authorized. 1991. $5-8.

Plastic bottle caps in original package. Authenticity questionable. 1970. $5-7.

Cash register. Version with Mr. Peanut on left. Not authorized. Fantasy item. 1989. Price not available.

Quart jar with Mr. Peanut needle point on lid. 1989. $5-8.

Wooden bowl with Mr. Peanut painted in bowl, believed to be part of a 3 bowl set, the others being a potato chip man and a pretzel man. 1960. $6-12.

Crochet Mr. Peanut doll. 14". Not
authentic. 1980s. $15-20.

Handmade cotton quilt. Fantasy piece.
39" x 60". $250 and up. 1988.

Plastic kazoo from Tonowanda, N.Y. 4.75". 1990. $4-6. Reproduction.

Cast iron Mr. Peanut Christmas stocking holder. #10 on bottom.
5.75". Not authorized. 1990s. $4-8.

Wooden Mr. Peanut with a spring on his
arm that raises it up and down as he
tips his hat. 8.5". Not authentic. 1980s.
$10-20.

Glass cups with embossed Mr. Peanut face and top hat. 1982. Not authorized. 1993.
Reproductions. $4-8.

Hand made peanut container. 9.25" x 10" high. Also available in red, brown or dark green. Fantasy item. 1993. $45-70.

Composite statue, much like the cast iron fence post sitter. 48" tall. 1981. $250-300.

Plastic dice with Mr. Peanut engraved on front. Available in several colors. 1990. $2-5 each set.

Wooden shelf with Mr. Peanut and Planters Peanuts written on front. 1990s. Not authorized. Fantasy item. $10-20.